TRADITIONS AND CELEBRATIONS

POWWOWS

by Katrina M. Phillips

PEBBLE
a capstone imprint

Published by Pebble, an imprint of Capstone
1710 Roe Crest Drive, North Mankato, Minnesota 56003
capstonepub.com

Copyright © 2026 by Capstone. All rights reserved. No part of this publication may be reproduced in whole or in part, or stored in a retrieval system, or transmitted in any form or by any means, electronic, mechanical, photocopying, recording, or otherwise, without written permission of the publisher.

Library of Congress Cataloging-in-Publication Data is available on the Library of Congress website.

ISBN: 9798875220050 (hardcover)
ISBN: 9798875220005 (paperback)
ISBN: 9798875220012 (ebook PDF)

Summary: Powwows are about dancing! Indigenous people in America hold powwows to celebrate their past and present. Drummers strike up the music, and dancers show off their best moves and fancy regalia. Indigenous people remember their history, honor their ancestors, and celebrate their heritage. Come and watch the dancers!

Editorial Credits
Editor: Kellie M. Hultgren; Designer: Elijah Blue; Media Researcher: Jo Miller; Production Specialist: Tori Abraham

Image Credits
Alamy: Charles Crust/ Danita Delimont, Agent, 19, ClassicStock/H. ARMSTRONG ROBERTS, 11, 13, Len Collection, 15; Getty Images: Bobbie DeHerrera/Newsmakers, 18, iStock/lessrob, 25, Norm Hall, 1; Granger: Agence Roger Viollet, 12; Shutterstock: Akerri, 9, Alina Reynbakh, 21, 24, Bill Perry, cover, Darlene Stanley, 8, HannaTor, 27, 28, Kobby Dagan, 29, Leonard Zhukovsky, 4, 17, MotionPixxle Studio, 23, Pierre Jean Durieu, 5, ThunderBirdEye, 7, Vicki L. Miller, 20

Design Elements
Shutterstock: Rafal Kulik

All internet sites appearing in back matter were available and accurate when this book was sent to press.

Printed and bound in China. 006276

TABLE OF CONTENTS

What Is a Powwow?..4

The History of Powwows 10

What Happens at a Powwow?...................14

Powwow Music 18

Powwow Dances 20

Proud to Be Indigenous 28

    Glossary...30

    Read More 31

    Internet Sites 31

    Index 32

    About the Author............................32

Words in **bold** are in the glossary.

What Is a Powwow?

Powwows are **Indigenous** gatherings. People come together to share Indigenous **traditions**. They honor their Elders and **veterans**.

Dancers at the United Tribes Pow Wow in Bismarck, North Dakota

The first powwows were held on the Great Plains. This area is east of the Rocky Mountains.

Today, powwows are held all across the country. Some people go to powwows close to home. Others travel to powwows in other places.

Powwows can be held in big cities or small towns. They can be held on **reservations** or at colleges. Some are very big. The He Sapa Wacipi Na Oskate is the Black Hills powwow. More than 18,000 people attend.

Dancers gather at the He Sapa Wacipi Na Oskate.

Powwows can have different names. Dakota, Lakota, and Nakota people call them wacipi (wa-CHEE-pee). This word means "they dance." Ojibwe people may call them ni-mi-win or niimi'idiwin. This comes from the Ojibwe word that means "a dance."

The Shakopee Mdewakanton Sioux Community Wacipi in Minnesota

Not all powwows are the same. But they all honor Indigenous ways of life.

The History of Powwows

Indigenous people have always danced. They have always found ways to gather together. But it was not always easy. The United States **banned** many Indigenous traditions in 1883.

The ban included dances. The government could arrest people for dancing. Dancers could go to jail. Government agents tore down Indigenous dance halls.

Men dance at the Gallup Inter-Tribal Ceremonial in New Mexico in the 1950s. This Indigenous cultural gathering started in 1922 and is still held today.

But Indigenous people still found ways to dance. They danced in secret. Some danced on the Fourth of July. Dancers would not be arrested for **celebrating** an American holiday. Others held dances at tribal fairs.

Artist Amos Bad Heart Bull drew this picture of the Oglala Lakota powwow of July 4, 1898.

Navajo women arrive at a corn dance at the Laguna Pueblo, New Mexico, in the 1930s.

People from other Indigenous nations came to these dances. They sang and danced together. Today, these events are known as powwows.

What Happens at a Powwow?

Many powwows begin with a Grand Entry. Flags are brought in. Everyone stands up to honor them.

The U.S. flag and the flags of tribal nations come in first. Military flags or state flags come next. Indigenous veterans usually carry these flags. Powwow dancers follow the flags into the arena.

Next are a Flag Song and an Honor Song. A Flag Song honors the American flag. It is sung in an Indigenous language. Some people dance in place. They are showing respect for a veteran in their family.

An Honor Song is for people who have done good things. Attendees stand up as a sign of respect. Then the powwow dances begin!

Powwow Music

Drum groups are an important part of powwows. Nobody could dance without them! A powwow may have several drum groups. Each group takes a turn.

Powwow drums are also called dance drums.

Drummers also sing the powwow songs. Some songs are very old. Others are new. Powwow songs are often sung in Indigenous languages.

Powwow drums have a wooden frame. An elk hide or buffalo hide is stretched over the frame.

Powwow Dances

There are many powwow dances. There are dances for men and dances for women. The dances can tell stories. They may remember history.

Some powwows have dances for children. Social dances are for everybody.

Men may be Traditional, Fancy, or Grass dancers. Grass Dance moves are like stomping down tall grass. The **ancestors** had to stomp down tall prairie grasses.

Men's Traditional dances honor the ancestors' warrior societies. The dances tell stories of hunting or tracking animals. The dancers use their heads and upper bodies to tell their stories.

A men's Fancy dancer

Women may be Traditional, Buckskin, or Ribbon dancers. They may be Fancy Shawl or Jingle Dress dancers too.

Girls perform a Jingle Dance.

Fancy Shawl dancer

Women did not always dance in the arena. Instead, they stood outside. They used their feet to keep time. Women's Traditional dancers step to the beat of the drum. They hold fans as they dance.

Some women are Fancy Shawl dancers. They wear a colorful shawl with fringe. They hold it out as they jump and turn.

Many powwow dancers wear special clothes called **regalia**. It is different for each style of dance. It can be decorated with beads, ribbons, or porcupine quills.

Each dancer's regalia is different. They may get it as a gift. They may make it. Or they may buy it from Indigenous makers.

Fancy Dance regalia is colorful. It may have feathers, quills, beads, and ribbons. It bobs and twirls as dancers move.

Proud to Be Indigenous

Indigenous people go to powwows for many reasons. They go to sing, dance, and drum. They go to honor their ancestors. They go to see family. They visit old friends and make new ones.

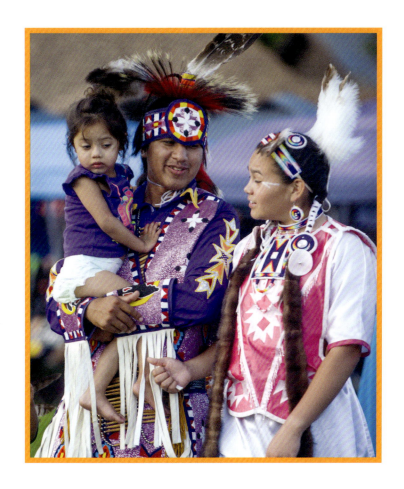

Indigenous people honor and celebrate their **cultures**. They learn and teach their languages. They teach new dancers and singers. They are proud of who they are. Powwows bring Indigenous people together.

GLOSSARY

ancestor (an-SEST-er)—a person from whom you are descended, like your great-grandparents

ban (BAN)—to legally stop someone from doing something

celebrating (SELL-a-brayt-ing)—marking an important holiday, event, or occasion

culture (KUHL-chur)—the traditions, beliefs, and behaviors that a group of people share

Indigenous (in-DIJ-eh-nus)—the first to live in a place

regalia (re-GALE-ee-uh)—special clothes that are worn for powwows or other special occasions

reservation (rez-er-VAY-shun)—land set aside for Indigenous nations

tradition (truh-DISH-un)—a custom or practice that is passed down from one generation to another

veteran (VET-er-run)—a person who has served in the military

READ MORE

Havrelock, Deidre. *Why We Dance: A Story of Hope and Healing.* New York: Abrams Books, 2024.

Sorell, Traci. *Powwow Day.* Watertown, MA: Charlesbridge Publishing, 2022.

Troian, Martha. *It's Powwow Time!* New York: Greenwillow Books, 2024.

INTERNET SITES

CBC Kids: Do You Know What a Powwow Is?
cbc.ca/kids/articles/do-you-know-what-a-powwow-is

CBC Kids News: "Explaining Powwow Culture: From Banned to Booming"
youtube.com/watch?v=V8LRK4iRVPI

Britannica Kids: Powwow
kids.britannica.com/kids/article/%20powwow/635015

INDEX

ancestors, 22, 28

banning, 10

clothing, 25, 26

dancing, 7, 8, 10–13, 20, 22, 24–26

drums, 18, 19, 25, 28

first powwows, 5, 10–13

flags, 14

gatherings, 10, 11

Grand Entry, 14

Indigenous history, 20

Indigenous languages, 16, 19, 29

New Mexico, 11, 13

regalia, 26

reservations, 6

songs, 16, 19

ABOUT THE AUTHOR

Dr. Katrina Phillips is a citizen of the Red Cliff Band of Lake Superior Ojibwe. She earned her BA and PhD from the University of Minnesota. She's a professor at Macalester College, where she teaches classes on Native history and the history of the American West.